SCARLATTI

The Five Fugues

'The Cat Fugue', Kp.30 & Kp.41, 58, 93, 417

Edited by

RICHARD JONES

THE ASSOCIATED BOARD OF
THE ROYAL SCHOOLS OF MUSIC

CONTENTS

INTRODUCTION

Only five harpsichord fugues of Scarlatti's have come down to us, but they are all substantial compositions; and in view of their generally similar style there seems to be a good case for uniting them in a single volume. By far the best-known is, of course, the Fugue in G minor, Kp.30 which, at some time long after the composer's death, became known as the 'Cat Fugue', perhaps because of the impression its subject gives of a cat stealthily climbing the sharps and flats of the keyboard. This piece forms the impressive culmination of Scarlatti's first published collection of harpsichord music, the *Essercizi* of 1738. Three other Fugues, Kp.41, 58 and 93 – according to Kirkpatrick – probably pre-date the *Essercizi*. They are, by Scarlatti's standards, thoroughly conventional in style, though none the worse for that. Their counterpoint flows smoothly – largely by step – and lies well under the hands. The approach to part-writing is very free, and the contrapuntal technique in general, as might be expected, closer to Handel's than to Bach's. Variations in thickness of texture are skilfully exploited, octave doublings in the L.H. used to good effect, and pedal points repeated rather than held due to the harpsichord's limited sustaining capacity. The single late fugue, Kp.417, exhibits the same general stylistic features, but towards the end (bb.107 ff.) we have a glimpse of the boldly original Scarlatti of the more idiomatic harpsichord music.

The sources of this edition are listed below; players who wish to consult them will find facsimiles in Vols I-III and XIV of Ralph Kirkpatrick's *Domenico Scarlatti: Complete Keyboard Works in Facsimile from the Manuscript and Printed Sources*, 18 vols, New York & London, 1972.

Kp.30 Source: ESSERCIZI PER GRAVICEMBALO/di/Don Domenico Scarlatti . . . [London, 1738]. Heading: SONATA . . . Fuga Moderato; key signature: one flat. The treble part in b.45 is ranged with quavers 2-6, but cf. the alto part in bb.5-6, etc.

Kp.41 Sources: A. Parma III (1752), No.30. B. XLII/Suites de Pieces/Pour le/ GLAVECIN./ . . . /Composées par/*Domenico Scarlatti*/ . . . /Thos Roseingrave./ LONDON/ . . . [1739]. Heading (both sources): Fuga And^{te} Moderato; key signature: no flat. This edition follows Source A in essentials, except at bb.14-16 (main text as B; *ossia* as A), last two alto notes of b.24 (A: *a' g'*) and first two of bb.76 & 77 (A: two crotchets), last bass note of b.86 (A: *c'*), and 3rd quaver of b.97 (A: no quav. *c''* natural).

Kp.58 Source: Venice XIV (1742), No.16. Heading: Sonata Fuga; key signature: two flats. The text is full of errors, among which are presumably to be numbered the many cases of parallel 5ths and 8ves. These have been corrected in this edition. The original readings are as follows: b.12: tenor doubles alto at an 8ve below; b.22, ten., 4th crotchet: crotchet *c'*; b.27, 3rd ten. note: *a* natural; b.39, 2nd alto note: *g'*; b.40, ten., 4th crotchet: *g*; b.41, 4th alto note: *g'*.

Kp.93 Source: Venice XIV (1742), No.60. Heading: Sonata Fuga; key signature: one flat.

Kp.417 Source: Parma X (1754), No.8. Heading: Fuga All^o Moderato.

The following conventions have been used to distinguish editorial markings from the composer's. Notes, rests and accidentals: small print; slurs and ties: ⌒⊢⌒ ; ornaments, staccatos, tempo markings and arpeggio signs: square brackets. In addition, the sign ⌊ / ⌈ denotes R.H./L.H.; [S], Subject entries; and commas, breaks in phrasing. All fingering is editorial.

RICHARD JONES
Oxford, 1985

FUGUE in G minor

'The Cat Fugue', Kp.30

SCARLATTI

[S] denotes Subject entries.

© 1986 by The Associated Board of the Royal Schools of Music

6

1) Crotchet dotted in the source.

1) Dotted crotchet *e* in the source.

1) Dotted crotchet chord in the source.

AB 1930

FUGUE in D minor

Kp.41

[S] denotes Subject entries.

12

1) Minim in the sources.

1) Minim in the sources.

FUGUE in C minor

Kp.58

[S] denotes Subject entries.

1) Plus two crotchet c's in the source, between alto and tenor; omitted here because unplayable.

Source readings: 1) Crotchet 2) Natural to *a'* 3) Flat to *g'* 4) *B* flat

AB 1930

Source readings: 1) Tenor, 3rd crotchet: *b* flat, *f*
2) Natural to *A*

AB 1930

FUGUE in G minor

Kp.93

[S] denotes Subject entries.

20

AB 1930

22

Source readings: 1) natural to *a'*; 2) natural to *e'*

FUGUE in D minor

Kp.417

[S] denotes Subject entries.

1) Tie across barline in the source.
2) *a*, not *b* flat, in the source.

1) Semibreve in the source.

1) *G*, not *A*, in the source.

Printed in England by Caligraving Limited Thetford Norfolk

AB 1930

11:95